FOOD LOVERS

TAPAS AND STARTERS

FOOD LOVERS

TAPAS AND STARTERS

RECIPES SELECTED BY CORINNE MALESIC

Trans
Atlantic
Press

All recipes serve four people, unless otherwise indicated.

For best results when cooking the recipes in this book, buy fresh ingredients and follow the instructions carefully. Make sure that everything is properly cooked through before serving, particularly any meat and shellfish, and note that as a general rule vulnerable groups such as the very young, elderly people, pregnant women, convalescents and anyone suffering from an illness should avoid dishes that contain raw or lightly cooked eggs.

For all recipes, quantities are given in metric measurements followed by standard U.S. cups and imperial measures. Follow one set or the other, but not a mixture of both because conversions may not be exact. Standard spoon and cup measurements are level and are based on the following:

1 tsp = 5 ml, 1 tbsp = 15 ml, 1 cup = 250 ml / 8 fl oz.

Note that Australian standard tablespoons are 20 ml, so Australian readers should use 3 tsp in place of 1 tbsp when measuring small quantities.

The electric oven temperatures in this book are given for conventional ovens with top and bottom heat. When using a fan oven, the temperature should be decreased by about 20–40ºF / 10–20ºC – check the oven manufacturer's instruction book for further guidance. The cooking times given should be used as an approximate guideline only.

CONTENTS

CARPACCIO OF BEEF

Ingredients

450 g / 1 lb beef tenderloin

1 tbsp creamed horseradish

Juice of 1 lemon

2 tbsp olive oil

Rock salt

Freshly crushed black pepper

50 g / ½ cup Parmesan cheese, shaved

1 handful arugula (rocket)

Method

Prep and cook time: 20 min plus 20 min chilling

1 Wrap the beef in plastic wrap (clingfilm) and place in the freezer for 20 minutes.

2 Slice the beef with a very sharp knife as thinly as possible and lay the slices on a serving platter or 4 individual plates.

3 Dot the creamed horseradish over the beef, drizzle over the lemon juice and oil and sprinkle with salt and pepper.

4 Scatter over the Parmesan cheese and arugula (rocket) and serve immediately.

BAKED PRUNES AND ALMONDS WRAPPED IN BACON

Ingredients

24 whole almonds, skinned

24 prunes, pitted

12 slices bacon, halved

2 tbsp oil

Method

Prep and cook time: 25 min

1 Heat the oven to 200C (400F / Gas Mark 6).

2 Place an almond in the cavity of each prune, wrap in a piece of bacon and secure with a wooden toothpick (cocktail stick).

3 Place the wrapped prunes on a cookie sheet, drizzle with the oil and bake for 10–15 minutes.

SPINACH AND TOMATO SALAD WITH HALLOUMI

Ingredients

150 ml / ⅔ cup olive oil

1 onion, cut into rings

250 g / 8 oz baby spinach

250 g / 8 oz cherry tomatoes, sliced

250 g / 8 oz yellow cherry tomatoes, sliced

50 g / 1 cup black olives, pitted

2 tbsp curly parsley, roughly chopped

Juice of 2 lemons

250 g / 8 oz halloumi cheese

Salt and freshly ground pepper

Method

Prep and cook time: 20 min

1 Heat 2 tbsp of the oil in a skillet (frying pan) and gently fry the onion rings until soft. Remove from the heat and set aside.

2 Mix together the spinach, tomatoes, olives, parsley and cooked onion rings.

3 Blend 6 tbsp of the oil with the lemon juice, season with salt and pepper, and dress the salad.

4 Heat the remaining oil in the skillet and fry the halloumi for 2 minutes, turning once, until lightly browned.

5 Place the halloumi on the salad and serve immediately.

POTATOES WITH TOMATO SAUCE

Ingredients

450 g / 1 lb small waxy potatoes, washed

4 tbsp olive oil

2 onions, cut into rings

1 garlic clove

1 red chili pepper, seeds removed and finely chopped

3 tbsp sherry

400 g / 2 cups canned tomatoes

7 tbsp vegetable broth (stock)

100 g / 1 cup black olives, pitted

4 tbsp pine nuts, dry roasted

Salt and freshly ground pepper

Method

Prep and cook time: 25 min

1 Boil the potatoes in salted water for about 20 minutes or until tender.

2 Meanwhile, heat the oil in a pan and gently fry the onion until translucent. Add the garlic and chili and cook for a further 2 minutes.

3 Pour in the sherry, allow to reduce a little then add the tomatoes and vegetable broth (stock). Simmer gently for 10 minutes then season with salt and pepper.

4 Serve the potatoes with the sauce poured over and topped with olives and pine nuts.

FILO PASTRIES
WITH SPINACH AND
GOAT CHEESE

Ingredients

675 g / 1½ lb spinach, washed and stalks discarded

3 tbsp olive oil

5 scallions (spring onions), finely chopped

¼ tsp grated nutmeg

200 g / 2 cups soft goat cheese, crumbled

450 g / 1 lb filo pastry, thawed if frozen

50 g / ¼ cup butter, melted

Salt and freshly ground pepper

Method

Prep and cook time: 40 min

1 Put the spinach in a large pan. Cover and cook until wilted then drain, squeezing out as much liquid as possible. Finely chop the leaves and set aside.

2 Heat the oil in a pan and gently cook the scallions (spring onions) until soft. Stir in the spinach, nutmeg and goat cheese and cook for 2 minutes. Drain off any liquid, season with salt and pepper and set aside.

3 Heat the oven to 180C (375F / Gas Mark 5).

4 Cut 15 cm x 6 cm (6 inch x 2½ inch) rectangles and brush with melted butter. Put a small spoonful of the mixture on the end of each rectangle and fold 3 times to make a triangular parcel.

5 Place the parcels on a greased baking sheet, brush with more melted butter and bake for 10–15 minutes. Serve hot or cold.

Makes 16

ONIONS STUFFED WITH GOAT CHEESE

Ingredients

300 g / 12 oz goat cheese, chopped

4 slices prosciutto, chopped

1 tbsp red peppercorns, crushed

1 tsp black peppercorns, crushed

4 bay leaves

4 garlic cloves, chopped

Zest and juice of 2 lemons

500 ml / 2 cups extra virgin olive oil

4 medium red onions

250 ml / 1 cup chicken broth (stock)

Thyme sprigs, to garnish

Method

Prep and cook time: 45 min plus 8 hours to marinate

1 Place the goat cheese in a bowl with the prosciutto, crushed peppercorns, bay leaves, garlic and lemon zest. Cover with the oil and lemon juice and refrigerate for 8 hours or overnight.

2 Heat the oven to 230C (450F / Gas Mark 8).

3 Peel the onions, cut off the tops and hollow out. Place the onions and their tops in a baking dish. Add the broth (stock) to the bottom of the dish, cover with foil and bake for 20 minutes until the onions are just soft. Remove from pan with a slotted spoon and set aside.

4 Preheat the broiler (grill) to a high heat. Remove the goat cheese from the refrigerator. Strain the liquid from the goat cheese; keep the spices, prosciutto and garlic, and discard the bay leaves.

5 Stuff the hollowed onions with the cheese/ prosciutto mixture and place in a shallow baking dish or pan. Cook under the broiler for 3 minutes or until the tops are golden brown. Garnish with thyme and serve.

SPICY FISHCAKES

Ingredients

300 g / 12 oz floury potatoes, peeled and roughly chopped

450 g / 1 lb skinned white fish fillets

250 ml / 1 cup milk

2 bay leaves

2 scallions (spring onions), finely chopped

1 red chili, seeds removed and finely chopped

150 g / $^2/_3$ cup corn kernels, finely chopped

1 tbsp cilantro (fresh coriander), finely chopped

1 egg, beaten

2 tbsp oil

1 tsp paprika

Salt and freshly ground pepper

Lime wedges, to serve

Method

Prep and cook time: 40 min

1 Boil the potatoes in a large pan of salted water until soft.

2 Meanwhile, put the fish fillets in a wide pan with the milk and bay leaves and simmer for 7 minutes or until the fish is cooked. Discard the bay leaves, reserve the milk and mash the fish flesh.

3 Mash the potatoes with a little of the reserved milk then add the mashed fish, scallions (spring onions), chili, corn, cilantro (fresh coriander) and egg, and season with salt and pepper.

4 With wet hands, shape the mixture into patties. Heat the oil in a skillet, stir in the paprika and fry the fish cakes for 3 minutes on each side or until browned. Serve with lime wedges.

EGGPLANT AND HALLOUMI ROLLS

Ingredients

1 red bell pepper, halved lengthways and seeds removed

150 ml / ⅔ cup olive oil

2 red chilis, seeds removed and finely chopped

1 garlic clove, finely chopped

2 medium eggplants (aubergines)

675 g / 1½ lb halloumi cheese, cut into thick slices

Salt and freshly ground pepper

Rosemary sprigs, to garnish

Method

Prep and cook time: 30 min

1 Heat the broiler (grill) to the highest setting. Brush the bell peppers with a little oil and place under the broiler skin sides up until the skin has blackened. Remove the skins and chop the flesh finely.

2 Heat 2 tbsp of oil in a pan and gently cook the chopped chili and garlic until soft. Add the chopped bell pepper, season with salt and pepper and set aside.

3 Cut the eggplants (aubergines) lengthways into ½ cm / ¼ inch slices.

4 Heat 3 tbsp of oil in a skillet and fry the eggplant slices in batches until they are golden brown. Drain on kitchen paper, set aside and keep warm.

5 Heat the remaining oil in the skillet and fry the sliced halloumi until browned. Season with salt and pepper.

6 Spoon a little of the chili mixture onto each halloumi slice, wrap in a slice of eggplant and secure with toothpicks (cocktail sticks).

7 Serve immediately garnished with the remaining chili sauce and the rosemary sprigs.

PROSCIUTTO AND MANGO SALAD

Ingredients

5 tbsp olive oil

3 tbsp white wine vinegar

½ tsp chili powder

150 g / 6 oz baby red spinach or beet tops, washed

1 small head radicchio, leaves separated and washed

4 sprigs parsley

1 large mango, peeled, stone removed and sliced

8 slices prosciutto, chopped into strips

Salt and freshly ground pepper

Method

Prep and cook time: 20 min

1 Mix the oil with the vinegar and chili powder, season with salt and pepper and set aside.

2 Arrange the spinach, radicchio leaves and parsley on serving plates.

3 Add the sliced mango and strips of prosciutto and drizzle with the dressing.

4 Serve with any remaining dressing alongside.

CALAMARI WITH LIME DRESSING

Ingredients

1 tbsp white wine vinegar

2 tbsp lime juice

3 tbsp light cream

5 tbsp olive oil

1 tbsp parsley, finely chopped

675 g / 1½ lb calamari rings, thawed if frozen

1 bunch arugula (rocket)

Salt and freshly ground pepper

Lime wedges

Method

Prep and cook time: 20 min

1 Mix the vinegar, lime juice, cream and 3 tbsp of oil to make the dressing. Stir in the parsley, season with salt and pepper and set aside.

2 Heat a griddle pan or broiler (grill) to medium heat. Wash the calamari rings and pat dry. Brush with the remaining oil and cook for about 4 minutes, turning once.

3 Serve the calamari on a bed of arugula (rocket) with the dressing drizzled over and lime wedges to garnish.

TARRAGON MUSHROOMS ON TOAST

Ingredients

4 tbsp butter

250 g / 8 oz button mushrooms

1 garlic clove, finely chopped

½ bunch tarragon, chopped

100 ml / 7 tbsp white wine

4 tbsp crème fraîche

4 slices baguette

Salt and freshly ground pepper

Tarragon leaves, to garnish

Method

Prep and cook time: 10 min

1 Heat the butter in a pan and cook the mushrooms for about 1 minute, or until golden brown.

2 Add the garlic and chopped tarragon, toss briefly and stir in the white wine. Boil until reduced, then stir in the crème fraîche and cook for about 1 minute.

3 Toast the baguette slices on both sides.

4 Season the mushrooms to taste with salt and pepper and place on the toasted baguette slices. Serve garnished with tarragon.

SHRIMPS WITH PESTO

Ingredients

2 tbsp olive oil

450 g / 1 lb shrimps, black
veins removed

4 basil leaves, shredded

2 limes, cut into wedges, to serve

For the pesto:

50 g / 2 oz basil leaves

2 tbsp Parmesan cheese, grated

2 tbsp pine nuts

125 ml / ½ cup olive oil

Salt

Method

Prep and cook time: 15 min

1 Put the pesto ingredients into a food processor and pulse until thoroughly blended. Season with salt and set aside.

2 Heat the oil in a skillet (frying pan) and fry the shrimps until pink and cooked through.

3 Drizzle the pesto over the shrimps, scatter with the shredded basil and serve with the lime wedges.

POTATO ROSTI
WITH SMOKED SALMON AND HERB CREAM CHEESE

Ingredients

250 g / 1 cup cream cheese

1 tbsp capers, drained and finely chopped

Small bunch of chives, finely chopped

1 tbsp parsley, finely chopped

Juice of 1 lemon

4 large potatoes, peeled

1 tbsp flour

3 tbsp olive oil

250 g / 8 oz smoked salmon, sliced

Salt and freshly ground pepper

Chives, to garnish

Method
Prep and cook time: 35 min

1 Beat the cream cheese with the capers, chives, parsley and lemon juice. Season with salt and pepper and set aside.

2 Boil the potatoes in a large pan of salted water for about 5 minutes. Drain well and let cool.

3 Grate the potatoes with a coarse grater, stir in the flour and season with salt and pepper.

4 Heat the oil in a wide skillet and gently fry spoonfuls of the potato mixture until golden brown. Drain on kitchen paper.

5 Serve the rostis with the herb cream cheese and smoked salmon, garnished with chives.

FRIED CHORIZO WITH TOMATO AND ONION SAUCE

Ingredients

6 large tomatoes

125 ml / ½ cup olive oil

250 g / ½ lb cooking chorizo, sliced

1 large onion, chopped

1 garlic clove

2 stalks thyme

Salt and freshly ground pepper

Method
Prep and cook time: 20 min

1 Bring a pan of salted water to a boil and drop in the tomatoes for 30 seconds. Remove from the water, peel and slice. Set aside.

2 Heat 4 tbsp of oil in a wide pan and fry the chorizo slices for about 5 minutes, turning once. Set aside.

3 Heat the remaining oil in the pan and gently cook the onion until soft. Add the garlic, cook for 2 minutes then add the tomatoes.

4 Cover the pan and simmer for 8 minutes, adding a little water if necessary.

5 Add the chorizo and the thyme sprigs and cook for a further 3 minutes. Season with salt and pepper and serve.

ROASTED PUMPKIN AND GORGONZOLA SALAD

Ingredients

1 medium pumpkin, peeled and seeds removed

150 ml / $^2/_3$ cup olive oil

2 tbsp balsamic vinegar

200 g / 8 oz baby spinach

325 g / 12 oz Gorgonzola, crumbled

Salt and freshly ground pepper

Method

Prep and cook time: 50 min

1 Heat the oven to 200C (400F / Gas Mark 6).

2 Cut the pumpkin into slim wedges and cut each in half. Brush with a little of the oil and place on a cookie sheet. Bake for 20–30 minutes or until tender. Remove from the oven and let cool.

3 Mix the remaining oil with the balsamic vinegar, season with salt and pepper and set aside.

4 Arrange the spinach on serving plates, add the cooked pumpkin and Gorgonzola, and drizzle over the balsamic dressing.

BAKED TOMATOES
WITH COUSCOUS
AND HERBS

Ingredients

150 g / 1 cup couscous

12 medium tomatoes

100 ml / 7 tbsp olive oil

3 scallions (spring onions),
finely chopped

2 red chilis, seeds removed and
finely chopped

1 tbsp basil, finely chopped

1 tbsp parsley, finely chopped

Salt and freshly ground pepper

Lettuce leaves, to serve

Method
Prep and cook time: 35 min

1 Cook the couscous according to the packet instructions, fluff with a fork and set aside.

2 Heat the oven to 200C (400F / Gas Mark 6).

3 Cut the tops off the tomatoes and carefully scoop out the seeds. Discard the seeds and chop the core flesh finely.

4 Heat 3 tbsp of oil in a pan and gently fry the scallions (spring onions) until soft. Add the chili and chopped tomato cores and cook for 2 minutes.

5 Stir the scallion mixture into the couscous, add the herbs and season with salt and pepper.

6 Brush the tomatoes inside and out with the remaining oil. Spoon the couscous mixture into the tomatoes, replace the tops and place on a baking sheet.

7 Bake for 15–20 minutes and serve on lettuce leaves with the pan juices spooned over.

SARDINE PÂTÉ WITH TOAST

Ingredients

240 g / ½ lb sardines, canned in oil

2 tbsp crème fraîche

Juice of 1 lemon

1 tbsp thyme leaves, chopped

1 tbsp parsley, chopped

Salt and freshly ground pepper

To serve:

Baguette slices, toasted

Celery, cut into strips

Method

Prep and cook time: 10 min

1 Put the sardines and the oil from the cans into a food processor.

2 Add the crème fraîche, lemon juice, thyme and parsley, and pulse until you have a coarse mixture.

3 Season with salt and pepper and serve with the toasted baguette slices and celery.

CHICKEN KEBABS
WITH PEANUT SAUCE

Ingredients

125 ml / ½ cup sesame oil

1 garlic clove, chopped

2 red chilis, chopped

2 tbsp honey

250 ml / 1 cup smooth peanut butter

1 tbsp soy sauce

1 tsp fish sauce

Juice of 2 limes

2 chicken breasts, skinned and sliced

1 tbsp light oil

Chilis and lime wedges, to garnish

Method
Prep and cook time: 25 min

1 Heat the oil in a small pan and gently cook the garlic and chilis until soft. Stir in the honey, peanut butter, soy sauce, fish sauce and lime juice. Bring to a boil and simmer for 5 minutes.

2 Thread the chicken strips onto wooden skewers and brush with a little oil.

3 Heat a griddle pan and cook the chicken skewers until browned and cooked through.

4 Serve the chicken skewers drizzled with the sauce, garnish with whole chilis and lime wedges, and serve the remaining sauce alongside for dipping.

PEARS WITH BLUE CHEESE AND WALNUTS

Ingredients

6 ripe pears

Juice of ½ a lemon

1 tbsp olive oil

200 g / 2 cups blue cheese, crumbled

150 g / 1½ cups walnuts, chopped

Rosemary sprigs, to garnish

Method

Prep and cook time: 15 min

1 Slice the pears in half lengthways and cut away the cores. Rub the cut surfaces with the lemon juice to prevent browning.

2 Heat the oil in a small pan and add the crumbled blue cheese and the walnuts.

3 Stir over a gentle heat until the cheese has just melted then spoon the mixture into the core cavities of the pears.

4 Serve immediately garnished with the rosemary.

GRILLED PEPPERS WITH GARLIC

Ingredients

6 long red bell peppers

125 ml / ½ cup olive oil

Juice of ½ a lemon

6 cloves new season garlic, roughly chopped

10 g / ½ cup parsley, roughly chopped

Salt and freshly ground pepper

Method

Prep and cook time: 40 min

1 Put the whole bell peppers under a hot broiler (grill), turning frequently, until the skins are charred all over.

2 Place the peppers in a large bowl, cover with plastic wrap (clingfilm) and let cool for 15 minutes.

3 Remove and discard the skins, stalks and seeds from the peppers.

4 Blend the olive oil with the lemon juice, season with salt and pepper, and mix well with the peppers.

5 Arrange on a serving plate and scatter with the garlic and parsley. For a gentler flavor, fry the garlic in a little olive oil until soft before adding to the dish. If no new season garlic is available, do the same with stored garlic.

TOMATO PUFF PASTRY TARTS

Ingredients

4 tbsp olive oil

4 garlic cloves, sliced

450 g / 1 lb all-butter puff pastry, thawed if frozen

450 g / 1 lb tomatoes, sliced

Salt and freshly ground pepper

Parsley, to garnish

Method

Prep and cook time: 40 min

1 Heat the oven to 180C (375F / Gas Mark 5).

2 Heat 3 tbsp of oil in a small pan and gently cook the garlic until softened.

3 Roll out the pastry to a thickness of 1 cm / ¼ inch, cut 10 cm / 4 inch diameter circles and place on a greased cookie sheet. Leaving a 1½ cm / ½ inch rim, score an inner circle on the pastry and carefully remove the top two layers of pastry from the inner circle.

4 Lay the sliced tomatoes in the middle of the tarts, scatter over the fried garlic and drizzle over the remaining oil.

5 Season with salt and pepper and bake for 15–20 minutes or until golden brown. Serve garnished with parsley.

PROSCIUTTO, MELON AND MOZZARELLA ROLLS

Ingredients

¼ Canteloupe melon, peeled and seeds removed

¼ Galia melon, peeled and seeds removed

12 slices prosciutto, cut into wide strips

450 g / 1 lb baby mozzarellas

2 tbsp basil, roughly chopped

4 tbsp sweet chili sauce

Method
Prep and cook time: 20 min

1 Chop the flesh of both melons into bite-size pieces.

2 Wrap each strip of prosciutto around a piece of each of the melons, a mozzarella ball, a piece of basil and a little of the chili sauce. Secure with toothpicks (cocktail sticks).

ARTICHOKES WITH RACLETTE CHEESE

Ingredients

4 globe artichokes

1 tbsp white wine vinegar

2 tbsp olive oil

2 garlic cloves, chopped

8 slices raclette cheese

1 tbsp chopped parsley

Salt and freshly ground pepper

Method

Prep and cook time: 35 min

1 Slice the artichokes in half vertically. Remove the tough outer leaves, peel the stalks and scrape out the hairy chokes with a teaspoon.

2 Bring a large pan of water to a boil with the vinegar and boil the prepared artichokes for 10–15 minutes or until tender. Drain well and set aside.

3 Heat the oven to 240C (475F / Gas Mark 9).

4 Place the artichokes cup side up in an ovenproof dish. Drizzle over the oil, scatter with the garlic and season with salt and pepper.

5 Lay one slice of cheese on each artichoke, sprinkle with the parsley and bake for 5 minutes or until the cheese is melted and golden brown. Serve hot or warm.

SHRIMP AND SCALLOPS WITH LIME SAUCE

Ingredients

Juice and zest of 4 limes

1 tbsp fish sauce

1 tsp sugar

8 scallops, with shells

3 tbsp olive oil

2 garlic cloves, finely chopped

1 red chili, seeds removed and finely chopped

8 large shrimps, tails and black veins removed

Method

Prep and cook time: 20 min

1 Mix the lime juice and zest with the fish sauce and sugar and set aside.

2 Cut the scallops away from the shell, discarding the corals. Rinse the scallops and shells and pat dry with kitchen paper. Slice each scallop in half horizontally and set aside.

3 Heat the oil in a skillet and gently fry the garlic and chili until just starting to soften. Remove the garlic and chili with a slotted spoon and add to the lime juice mixture.

4 Place the scallops cut side down in the skillet and cook for 1 minute on each side. Remove from the skillet and add to the lime juice mixture.

5 Heat the skillet again, quickly fry the shrimps until cooked through and add to the lime and scallop mixture.

6 Place two halves of a scallop on each shell along with one shrimp and pour over the lime mixture.

AVOCADO AND CRABMEAT

Ingredients

125 ml / ½ cup olive oil

1 tbsp Dijon mustard

Juice of 1 lemon

1 tsp honey

450 g / 1 lb crabmeat

2 punnets daikon cress

2 avocados

Salt and freshly ground pepper

Pink peppercorns, to garnish

Method

Prep and cook time: 20 min

1 Mix 3 tbsp of the oil with the mustard, lemon juice and honey to make a dressing and season with salt and pepper.

2 Mix the dressing with the crabmeat and set aside.

3 Cut the cress from the punnets and set aside a few sprigs to garnish. Whizz the remaining cress and oil in a blender and set aside.

4 Put small piles of the crabmeat onto serving plates. Peel the avocados, remove the stones and slice the flesh.

5 Lay the avocado slices over the crabmeat, drizzle over the cress oil and garnish with reserved cress leaves and crushed pink peppercorns.

CHICKEN WITH BELL PEPPER SAUCE

Ingredients

125 ml / ½ cup oil

Juice of 2 limes

2 tbsp honey

1 red chili, seeds removed and chopped

2 chicken breasts, skinned

2 orange bell peppers

1 garlic clove

Salt and freshly ground pepper

Lime zest, to garnish

Method

Prep and cook time: 45 min

1 Whisk together 6 tbsp of oil with the lime juice, honey and chopped chili to make a marinade.

2 Cut the chicken into bite-size pieces, mix with the marinade and set aside.

3 Brush the bell peppers with a little oil and place under a hot broiler (grill) until the skins are charred all over, turning frequently. Put in a bowl, cover with plastic wrap (clingfilm) and set aside.

4 Heat 2 tbsp of oil in a pan and gently fry the garlic for 2 minutes.

5 Remove and discard the pepper skins and seeds. Place the peppers in a food processor with the garlic and blend well. Season with salt and pepper and set aside.

6 Remove the chicken from the marinade. Heat the remaining oil in a skillet and fry the chicken pieces for about 6 minutes or until browned on all sides and cooked through.

7 Mix the peppers and garlic with the reserved marinade, heat quickly in the skillet and drizzle over the chicken pieces. Scatter with lime zest and serve immediately.

POTATOES BAKED IN SALT
WITH SOUR CREAM AND 'CAVIAR'

Ingredients

12 small new potatoes

2 tbsp olive oil

250 g / 8 oz rock salt

250 ml / 1 cup soured cream

125 g / 4 oz salmon caviar or lump fish roe

Zest of two lemons

Dill sprigs, to garnish

Method

Prep and cook time: 1 hour

1 Heat the oven to 180C (375F / Gas Mark 5).

2 Wash the potatoes thoroughly and rub with the oil.

3 Scatter the rock salt onto a baking sheet and place the potatoes on top. Bake in the oven for 45 minutes or until the potatoes are tender.

4 Scatter the salt onto a serving dish. Slice open the potatoes, place onto the serving dish and spoon a little soured cream into each one.

5 Top the potatoes with the fish roe, drizzle over any remaining cream, scatter over the lemon zest and garnish with dill sprigs.

OLIVE AND HAM BREAD CUBES

Ingredients

225 g / 8 oz bread flour, plus extra for kneading

7 g / 1 tsp easy blend yeast

1 tsp salt

2 tsp sugar

150 ml / $^2/_3$ cup water, lukewarm

2 tbsp olive oil

100 g / 1 cup olives stuffed with pimento, drained and sliced

100 g / 4 oz cooked ham, chopped

Method

Prep and cook time: 1 hour 15 min

1 Sift the flour into a bowl with the yeast, salt and sugar.

2 Add the water and oil and mix to form a dough. Turn onto a floured board and knead for 5 minutes. Return to the bowl, cover and leave in a warm place to rise for 30 minutes.

3 Heat the oven to 220C (425F / Gas Mark 7).

4 Turn the dough onto a floured board and knead for 10 minutes. Stretch the dough across the board, sprinkle over the olives and ham and knead for 2 more minutes.

5 Spread the dough into a greased roasting pan about 20 cm × 25 cm (8 inches × 10 inches) in size, brush with a little oil and bake for 25–30 minutes until risen and golden brown.

6 Turn out the bread, slice off the crusts and cut into bite-size squares.

RED ONION AND OLIVE BRUSCHETTAS

Ingredients

4 tbsp olive oil

4 red onions, finely sliced

2 garlic cloves, finely chopped

2 tomatoes, seeds removed and chopped

50 g / ½ cup black olives, pitted and sliced

1 tbsp balsamic vinegar

8 slices baguette, toasted

2 tbsp basil leaves, shredded, to garnish

Method

Prep and cook time: 20 min

1 Heat the oil in a pan and gently cook the onions until soft.

2 Add the garlic and tomatoes, cook for 2 minutes then stir in the olives and balsamic vinegar.

3 Spread the onion mixture onto the toasted baguette slices and serve immediately garnished with the basil.

LAMB PASTIES

Ingredients

For the pastry:

50 g / ¼ cup butter, chopped

250 g / 2½ cups all-purpose (plain) flour

3 tbsp olive oil

½ tsp salt

For the filling:

3 tbsp oil

1 onion, finely chopped

2 garlic cloves, chopped

250 g / 9 oz ground (minced) lamb

150 g / 1½ cups feta cheese, crumbled

1 tbsp pine nuts, chopped

2 egg yolks

Oil, for brushing

Salt and freshly ground pepper

Method

Prep and cook time: 50 min

1 Rub the butter into the flour until the mixture resembles breadcrumbs. Add the oil, salt and enough water to make a dough. Wrap in plastic wrap (clingfilm) and chill for 20 minutes.

2 Meanwhile, make the filling. Heat the oil in a pan and gently cook the onion until translucent. Add the garlic and lamb and cook, stirring, until the meat is well browned.

3 Remove from the heat and stir in the feta cheese, pine nuts and egg yolks. Season with salt and pepper and set aside.

4 Heat the oven to 180C (375F / Gas Mark 5).

5 Roll out the pastry thinly and cut circles about 10 cm/4 inches in diameter with a cutter. Place a little filling on each circle, moisten the edge with a little water, fold over to form semi-circles and press the join closed with a fork.

6 Place the pasties on a greased cookie sheet, brush with a little oil and bake for 15–20 minutes or until golden brown.

Makes 20

CHEESE SOUFFLÉS

Ingredients

100 g / ½ cup butter, softened

50 g / 1 cup fresh breadcrumbs

5 eggs, separated

150 g / 1½ cup cheese, Emmental or Gruyere, grated

4 tbsp heavy (double) cream

2 tbsp crème fraîche

2 tbsp flour

½ tsp paprika

Pinch nutmeg

Salt and freshly ground pepper

Method

Prep and cook time: 40 min

1 Grease 4 individual ramekins or ovenproof tea cups with a little of the butter and sprinkle the breadcrumbs over the buttered surfaces.

2 Heat the oven to 200C (400F / Gas Mark 6).

3 Beat the egg yolks and remaining butter together with the cheese, cream, crème fraîche, flour, paprika and nutmeg. Season with salt and pepper.

4 Whisk the egg whites until they form stiff peaks and fold into the egg yolk and cheese mixture.

5 Spoon into the ramekins and bake for 10–15 minutes or until golden brown and well risen.

MUSHROOM BRUSCHETTAS

Ingredients

4 tbsp olive oil

1 small onion, finely chopped

1 garlic clove, crushed

200 g / 2 cups button mushrooms, finely chopped

50 g / 1 cup black olives, pitted and finely chopped

12 slices baguette, toasted

Salt and freshly ground pepper

2 tbsp parsley, finely chopped, to garnish

Method

Prep and cook time: 25 min

1 Heat 3 tbsp of oil in a pan and gently fry the onion until soft.

2 Add the garlic, cook for 1 minute then add the mushrooms and cook for 10 minutes. Stir in the olives and season with salt and pepper.

3 Brush the toasted bread with the remaining oil, spoon over the mushroom mixture and garnish with the chopped parsley.

ASPARAGUS WRAPPED IN PARMA HAM

Ingredients

20 asparagus spears

50 g / ¼ cup butter, melted

10 slices Parma ham, sliced in half lengthways

Salt

Method

Prep and cook time: 15 min

1 Trim the bases off the asparagus and boil in a large pan of salted water for 4 minutes or until just tender.

2 Drizzle the asparagus with the melted butter and roll each one up in a strip of Parma ham.

ZUCCHINI FRITTERS

Ingredients

5 tbsp olive oil

1 onion, finely chopped

4 zucchini (courgettes), grated

4 tbsp all-purpose (plain) flour

Salt and freshly ground pepper

Method
Prep and cook time: 30 min

1 Heat 2 tbsp of oil in a pan and gently fry the onion until soft.

2 Mix the onion with the grated zucchini (courgettes) and the flour, season with salt and pepper and shape into small patties.

3 Heat the remaining oil in a skillet and fry the fritters for 3 minutes on each side or until golden brown.

4 Drain on kitchen paper and serve immediately.

CHICKPEA SALAD WITH SATAY CHICKEN SKEWERS

Ingredients

3 tbsp smooth peanut butter

125 ml / ½ cup olive oil

1 tbsp honey

Juice of 1 lime

2 chicken breasts, skinned and cut into strips

800 g / 4 cups canned chickpeas, drained and rinsed

2 red onion, finely chopped

2 red chilis, seeds removed and finely chopped

25 g / 1 cup chopped parsley

Juice of 1 lemon

Salt and freshly ground pepper

Method

Prep and cook time: 15 min plus 30 to marinate

1 Blend the peanut butter with 2 tbsp of oil, the honey and the lime juice. Pour over the chicken strips, mix well and set aside for 30 minutes.

2 Mix the chickpeas with the chopped onion, chilis and parsley. Mix the remaining oil with the lemon juice, season with salt and pepper and pour over the chickpeas.

3 Remove the chicken strips from the marinade and thread onto wooden skewers.

4 Cook the chicken under a hot broiler (grill) for 5 minutes or until cooked through, turning once. Serve with the chickpea salad.

SHRIMP AND TOMATO KEBABS WITH THAI SAUCE

Ingredients

6 tbsp soy sauce

2 tbsp fish sauce

3 tbsp sesame oil

Juice of 2 limes

2 tbsp honey

2 red chilis, seeds removed and finely chopped

2 garlic cloves, finely chopped

2 scallions (spring onions), finely chopped

675 g / 1½ lb large shrimps (prawns), tails and black veins removed

450 g / 1 lb cherry tomatoes, halved

Lime wedges, to garnish

Method

Prep and cook time: 20 min plus 30 min to marinate

1 Mix the soy sauce, fish sauce, 2 tbsp of sesame oil, the lime juice and honey in a large bowl.

2 Add the chopped chilis, garlic and scallions (spring onions) and mix in the shrimps (prawns). Set aside to marinate for 30 minutes, turning from time to time.

3 Heat the broiler (grill) to a medium setting.

4 Remove the shrimps from the marinade, brush the tomato halves with the remaining oil and thread onto wooden skewers alternating with the shrimps.

5 Heat the marinade in a small pan until reduced and slightly sticky. Set aside.

6 Cook the kebabs under the broiler, turning frequently, for about 6 minutes or until the shrimps are cooked through.

7 Serve the kebabs with the warm marinade drizzled over and lime wedges to garnish.

MINI QUICHES WITH HAM AND ARTICHOKES

Ingredients

110 g / ½ cup cold butter, chopped

225 g / 2½ cups all-purpose (plain) flour, plus extra for rolling

½ tsp salt

3 tbsp olive oil

1 onion, finely chopped

200 g / 8 oz pancetta or bacon, chopped

5 eggs

4 canned artichoke hearts, drained and chopped

Salt and freshly ground pepper

Method

Prep and cook time: 45 min

1 Rub the butter into the flour and salt until the mixture resembles breadcrumbs and add just enough iced water to form a dough. Wrap in plastic wrap (clingfilm) and set aside.

2 Heat the oven to 200C (400F / Gas Mark 6).

3 Heat the oil in a skillet (frying pan) and gently cook the onion until soft. Add the pancetta and cook for 3 minutes until just browned.

4 Put the eggs in a bowl and beat then stir in the onion / pancetta mixture and the artichokes. Season with salt and pepper and set aside.

5 Roll out the pastry on a floured board to a thickness of ½ cm / ¼ inch and cut 4 x 10 cm / 4 inch circles with a cutter.

6 Grease 4 x 8 cm / 3 inch tart tins and line with the pastry circles. Pour in the filling and bake for 10–15 minutes or until browned.

MUSSELS WITH PESTO

Ingredients

900 g / 2 lb mussels, scraped clean
and beards removed

125 ml / ½ cup white wine

25 g / 1 oz Parmesan cheese, grated

For the pesto:

50 g / 2 oz basil leaves

2 tbsp pine nuts

1 garlic clove, crushed

2 tbsp Parmesan cheese, grated

125 ml / ½ cup olive oil

Salt and freshly ground pepper

Method

Prep and cook time: 40 min

1 First make the pesto: pulse the basil, pine nuts and garlic in a food processor, or pound in a pestle and mortar, until coarsely chopped. Stir in the Parmesan cheese and olive oil and season with salt and pepper.

2 Tap each mussel against the side of the sink as you wash them and discard any that remain open.

3 Place the mussels in a large pan with the white wine and half a cup of water. Cover with a lid and cook over a medium heat for about 7 minutes, shaking the pan from time to time. Discard any mussels that remain closed after cooking.

4 Heat the oven to 220C (425F / Gas Mark 7).

5 Break off the top shell of each mussel and discard. Place the mussels on an ovenproof serving dish and spoon a little pesto onto each one. Sprinkle with the grated Parmesan cheese and heat in the oven for 3 minutes.

SCALLOPS WITH PROSCIUTTO, PARMESAN, ZUCCHINI AND HERB OIL

Ingredients

6 tbsp olive oil

2 zucchini (courgettes), sliced

6 large scallops, sliced in
half horizontally

4 slices prosciutto, sliced

50 g / 2 oz Parmesan cheese, shaved

Lemon wedges, to serve

For the herb oil:

Large handful mixed fresh herbs,
parsley, basil, thyme

125 ml / ½ cup olive oil

Juice of 1 lemon

Salt and freshly ground pepper

Method

Prep and cook time: 30 min

1 First make the herb oil: place the herbs in a blender with the oil and lemon juice and whiz until smooth. Season with salt and pepper and set aside.

2 Heat 3 tbsp of oil in a skillet and gently fry the zucchini (courgettes) until tender. Remove from the pan and set aside.

3 Heat the remaining oil in the skillet and cook the scallops for 2 minutes on each side or until browned.

4 Lay the zucchini onto serving dishes and drizzle with the herb oil. Add the scallops, prosciutto and Parmesan cheese, and serve with lemon wedges.

HONEY AND MUSTARD CHICKEN WINGS WITH SESAME SEEDS

Ingredients

3 tbsp olive oil

4 tbsp honey

2 tbsp Dijon mustard

Juice of 1 lemon

12 chicken wings

4 tbsp sesame seeds

Salt and freshly ground pepper

Method

Prep and cook time: 30 min plus 1 hour to marinate

1 Whisk together the oil, honey, mustard and lemon juice. Season with salt and pepper.

2 Put the chicken wings into a large bowl, pour over the marinade and mix well. Set aside for at least 1 hour, turning from time to time.

3 Heat the oven to 200C (400F / Gas Mark 6).

4 Toast the sesame seeds in a dry skillet until lightly browned. Set aside.

5 Remove the chicken wings from the marinade and put onto a cookie sheet. Roast in the oven for 15–20 minutes, turning once, until cooked through and browned all over.

6 Sprinkle the chicken wings with the toasted sesame seeds and serve warm or cold.

MEATBALLS
WITH TOMATO *SAUCE*

Ingredients

For the sauce:

2 tbsp olive oil

1 onion, finely chopped

1 garlic clove, finely chopped

1 bay leaf

400 g / 2 cups canned tomatoes, chopped

1 tbsp tomato paste (purée)

Salt and freshly ground pepper

For the meatballs:

1 slice white bread, soaked in a little water

450 g / 1 lb ground (minced) beef

1 egg, beaten

1 garlic clove, crushed

2 red chilis, seeds removed and finely chopped

1 onion, finely chopped

1 tsp dried thyme

2 tbsp chopped parsley

Salt and freshly ground pepper

Oil, for frying

1 garlic clove, finely chopped, to serve (optional)

Method

Prep and cook time: 40 min

1 To make the sauce, heat the oil in a pan and gently fry the onion until translucent.

2 Add the garlic, cook for 1 minute then add the bay leaf, tomatoes and tomato paste (purée). Stir in half a cup of water and let simmer for 15–20 minutes. Season with salt and pepper and remove from the heat.

3 Meanwhile, make the meatballs. Squeeze the excess liquid out of the bread and mix with the other meatball ingredients. Season with salt and pepper and shape into balls.

4 Heat 2 tbsp of oil in a skillet and fry the meatballs for about 10 minutes, shaking the skillet so they cook on all sides. Add more oil as necessary.

5 Remove the bay leaf from the sauce and discard. Spoon a little sauce into paper cases and top with a meatball. Serve garnished with raw chopped garlic (optional).

STUFFED ZUCCHINI FLOWERS

Ingredients

12 zucchini (courgette) flowers

450 g / 1 lb ricotta cheese

4 tbsp breadcrumbs

½ tsp grated nutmeg

2 eggs, beaten

100 g / 4 oz Parmesan cheese, grated

100 ml / 7 tbsp olive oil

Salt and freshly ground pepper

Method

Prep and cook time: 30 min plus 1 hour to marinate

1 Heat the oven to 220C (425F / Gas Mark 7).

2 Rinse the zucchini (courgette) flowers very carefully and pat dry with kitchen paper.

3 Mix the ricotta cheese with the breadcrumbs, nutmeg, beaten eggs and Parmesan cheese and season with salt and pepper.

4 Stuff the ricotta mixture into the middle of the zucchini flowers, gently twisting the petals to ensure that the stuffing doesn't fall out.

5 Pour 4 tbsp of oil into a roasting pan, place the stuffed zucchini flowers on top and drizzle over the remaining oil.

6 Bake in the oven for about 15 minutes, basting once during cooking. Serve the zucchini flowers with the pan juices drizzled over and season with salt and pepper.

PAPRIKA CHICKEN
WITH ONIONS

Ingredients

6 tbsp olive oil

1 onion, finely diced

1 garlic clove, chopped

1 tsp paprika

2 chicken breasts, skinned and cut into bite-size pieces

1 tbs balsamic vinegar

Cilantro (fresh coriander) sprigs, to garnish

Method

Prep and cook time: 20 min

1 Heat the oil in a pan and gently fry the onion until translucent. Add the garlic and paprika and cook for 1 more minute.

2 Turn up the heat, add the chicken pieces and cook for about 6 minutes, stirring frequently, until the chicken is browned and cooked through.

3 Add the balsamic vinegar, stir and cook for a further 2-3 minutes. Serve immediately, with cilantro (fresh coriander) to garnish.

MARINATED BELL PEPPERS WITH ANCHOVIES

Ingredients

6 red bell peppers

6 tbsp olive oil

2 garlic cloves, chopped

Juice of 1 lemon

100 g / 4 oz canned anchovies, drained

4 sprigs flat-leaf parsley, roughly chopped

Salt and freshly ground pepper

Method

Prep and cook time: 30 min plus 1 hour to marinate

1 Heat the broiler (grill) to a medium setting and broil (grill) the whole bell peppers, turning frequently, until the skins are charred all over.

2 Put the bell peppers into a bowl, cover with plastic wrap (cling film) and let cool.

3 Carefully remove and discard the pepper skins, discard the seeds and stem and slice the flesh.

4 Mix the oil, garlic and lemon juice. Season with salt and pepper.

5 Mix the peppers with the anchovies and chopped parsley, pour over the garlic and lemon marinade and mix well.

6 Set aside to marinate for at least 1 hour, turning the mixture from time to time.

POTATO TORTILLA

Ingredients

4 medium waxy potatoes, peeled

6 eggs

1 tbsp thyme, finely chopped

2 tbsp parsley, finely chopped

4 tbsp olive oil

Salt and freshly ground pepper

Method

Prep and cook time: 50 min

1 Boil the potatoes in a large pan of salted water until just tender. Let cool a little, cut in half lengthways and slice.

2 Beat the eggs in a large bowl, add the herbs, season with salt and pepper and add the sliced potatoes.

3 Heat 2 tbsp of oil over a medium flame in a 20 cm / 8 inch skillet (frying pan) and pour in half the egg / potato mixture.

4 Let cook for about 3 minutes then place a large plate over the pan, carefully invert and slide the tortilla, uncooked side down, back into the skillet.

5 Continue cooking for 2 more minutes or until the mixture is set then remove the tortilla from the pan.

6 Repeat with the remaining oil and egg / potato mixture. Slice the tortillas and serve warm or cold.

Published by Transatlantic Press

First published in 2011

Transatlantic Press
38 Copthorne Road, Croxley Green, Hertfordshire WD3 4AQ

© Transatlantic Press

Images and Recipes by StockFood © The Food Image Agency

Recipes selected by Corinne Malesic, StockFood

A catalogue record for this book is available from the British Library.

ISBN 978-907176-50-0

Printed in China